NEW VANGUARD 351

TANKS IN THE CAUCASUS 1942–43

WILLIAM E. HIESTAND ILLUSTRATED BY STEVE NOON

AF729777

OSPREY PUBLISHING
Bloomsbury Publishing Plc
Kemp House, Chawley Park, Cumnor Hill, Oxford OX2 9PH, UK
Bloomsbury Publishing Ireland Limited,
29 Earlsfort Terrace, Dublin 2, D02 AY28, Ireland
1385 Broadway, 5th Floor, New York, NY 10018, USA
E-mail: info@ospreypublishing.com
www.ospreypublishing.com

OSPREY is a trademark of Osprey Publishing Ltd

First published in Great Britain in 2026

© Osprey Publishing Ltd, 2026

All rights reserved. No part of this publication may be: i) reproduced or transmitted in any form, electronic or mechanical, including photocopying, recording or by means of any information storage or retrieval system without prior permission in writing from the publishers; or ii) used or reproduced in any way for the training, development or operation of artificial intelligence (AI) technologies, including generative AI technologies. The rights holders expressly reserve this publication from the text and data mining exception as per Article 4(3) of the Digital Single Market Directive (EU) 2019/790

A catalog record for this book is available from the British Library.

ISBN: PB 9781472870179; eBook 9781472870148;
ePDF 9781472870155; XML 9781472870162

26 27 28 29 30 10 9 8 7 6 5 4 3 2 1

Index by Sharon Redmayne
Typeset by Lumina Datamatics Ltd
Printed by Repro India Ltd.

MIX
Paper
FSC FSC® C047271

Title page caption: The dash for the oil fields, summer 1942. PzKpfw IIIs of the 23rd Panzer Division, up-gunned with the longer 50mm KwK 39 L/60 gun, drive south through the desert-like Caucasus region towards the oil fields of Maikop, Grozny, and Baku. Panzers driving through the arid terrain north of the mountains could be easily mistaken for Rommel's tanks in North Africa. (Nik Cornish at www.Stavka.photos)

Osprey Publishing supports the Woodland Trust, the UK's leading woodland conservation charity.

To find out more about our authors and books visit **www.ospreypublishing.com**. Here you will find extracts, author interviews, details of forthcoming events and the option to sign up for our newsletter.

For product safety-related questions, contact productsafety@bloomsbury.com

CONTENTS

INTRODUCTION 4

DOCTRINE AND ORGANIZATION 5

- German doctrine and organization
- Soviet doctrine and organization

TECHNICAL FACTORS 12

- German tanks and AFVs
- Soviet tanks and AFVs

THE CAMPAIGN 28

- Hitler's drive for oil, July–November 1942
- Retreat from the Caucasus, December 1942 to January 1943
- Stalemate in the Kuban, February–October 1943

ANALYSIS 44

FURTHER READING 46

INDEX 48

TANKS IN THE CAUCASUS 1942–43

INTRODUCTION

1942 saw Hitler's last successful *Blitzkrieg* offensives, with battle-hardened panzer divisions driving towards Stalingrad, the Caucasus oil fields, and the Suez Canal. Soviet and British tankers were initially unable to check the Wehrmacht, now equipped with numbers of *Panzerkampfwagen* (PzKpfw) IIIs and IVs carrying improved long 50 and 75mm guns, and by late summer it appeared that Germany's objectives were within reach.

Of the three thrusts, the drive for the Caucasus was Hitler's primary strategic focus for 1942. German intelligence estimated that the Maikop, Grozny, and Baku oil fields produced 70 percent of the Soviet Union's supplies, and their capture would cripple the USSR while fueling the Axis war effort. The ensuing clashes between Red Army and Wehrmacht tank units in the Caucasus were unusual for the Eastern Front. Due to heavy Red Army tank losses earlier in the summer, the panzers – almost always outnumbered by their Soviet opponents – for once began the campaign with more tanks than the defenders of the oil fields. The Soviets strove to rebuild

A German soldier examining a destroyed T-34 in the Kharkov area, May 28, 1942. By early 1942, the USSR rebuilt much of its tank inventory after the huge losses of the year before, but several thousand were lost during the disastrous Second Battle of Kharkov in May and during the early weeks of the Wehrmacht's Operation *Fall Blau* offensive. As a result, the Red Army defending the Caucasus was left with only a handful of operational tanks. (Photo by Keystone-France/Gamma-Keystone via Getty Images)

their tank brigades and battalions during the fall. Yet with little access to the steady stream of T-34s sent to other sectors of the front, they had to rely on Lend-Lease tanks – shipped via the Persian Gulf to the Caucasus – to an unusual degree. Just as in the Egyptian desert, in the arid steppes of the Caucasus, Valentines, M3 Lees, and M3 Stuarts battled to halt the panzer divisions.

DOCTRINE AND ORGANIZATION

German doctrine and organization

Although the armor and firepower of the British, French, and Soviet tanks they faced during the first years of the war was often superior, German panzer units prevailed through their superior doctrine, organization, and tactical expertise. Deep penetrations by panzer and motorized divisions, with strong Luftwaffe support, repeatedly encircled large enemy forces, leaving the pockets to be destroyed by the following hard-marching infantry armies. Panzer divisions were sophisticated combined-arms formations that in 1942 normally controlled a panzer regiment with two to three battalions, and two motorized infantry regiments each with two battalions. Supporting units included strong reconnaissance and motorcycle battalions, and motorized artillery, antitank, engineer, and supply elements. Panzer divisions typically had a company or battalion of their infantry mounted in *Schützenpanzerwagen* (SPW) half-tracks, although the majority were transported by truck throughout the war.

Although formally structured in separate regiments, in battle each division organized its panzers and motorized infantry along with other supporting units in combined-arms *Kampfgruppen* (battlegroups). Experienced leaders and staffs at all levels and excellent communication networks gave the *Kampfgruppen* a high level of battlefield flexibility, and the panzer divisions proved equally capable of assault, exploitation, mobile defense, and counterattack operations. During the *Blitzkrieg* years, the panzers usually operated under a specialized panzer army headquarters, each controlling several panzer corps with a mix of panzer and motorized divisions, often along with lesser numbers of infantry divisions and corps.

Spearheaded by the panzers, the Wehrmacht achieved a series of swift victories in Poland, France, and the Balkans. The opening months of Operation *Barbarossa* (Germany's invasion of the Soviet Union) saw stunning advances deep into the USSR, but the offensive ground to a halt before Leningrad, Moscow, and Rostov-on-Don late in the year. The panzer force on the Eastern Front suffered heavy attrition during the fighting, with only 1,015 tanks available at the beginning of 1942, many of them non-operational due to battle damage or mechanical breakdown. German tank

A panzer battalion deploys for action as it enters a pass in the Caucasus Mountains, while supporting infantry covers the advance from an overlooking hill. Panzer divisions were organized and trained to operate with their infantry, tanks, and artillery integrated in powerful combined arms *Kampfgruppen* (battlegroups). (National Digital Archives of Poland/Public Domain)

A PzKpfw III passes an 88mm antiaircraft gun during the Caucasus campaign. The 88mm was one of the few German guns that could reliably penetrate the T-34's and KV-1's frontal armor. The panzers often maneuvered to lure enemy armor into antitank kill-zones. (Nik Cornish at www.Stavka.photos)

production rates were modest, and in addition to the Eastern Front, tanks were sent to North Africa, while others equipped units posted from France to Norway. Due to the losses the year before, Germany was unable to launch another theater-wide offensive in 1942, and Hitler narrowed his objectives to the Soviet oil fields of the Caucasus. The panzer force in the east was built up to over 2,700 tanks, with Army Group South receiving the bulk of the replacements. Army Group North's and Center's panzer divisions each gave up one of its tank battalions to the nine divisions in the south assigned to the summer offensive, giving these three tank battalions each. By the summer of 1942, only 11 of the 25 panzer divisions approached full strength, two of them with Rommel in North Africa and the remaining nine – the 3rd, 9th, 11th, 13th, 14th, 16th, 22nd, 23rd, and 24th – with Army Group South.

The 1942 panzer battalion was formally organized according to a November 1941 table of organization. The battalion included two PzKpfw III companies, each with three five-tank platoons, two headquarters PzKpfw IIIs, and an additional reconnaissance platoon of five PzKpfw IIs. The battalion also had a PzKpfw IV company with two headquarters tanks, two or three four-tank platoons, and another five-PzKpfw II reconnaissance platoons. The table of organization strength for a panzer division was over 200 tanks, including up to 74 PzKpfw IIs, 106 IIIs, 42 IVs, and eight PzBfWg (*Panzerbefehlswagen*) command tanks, but even the high-priority Army Group South divisions did not reach these numbers. PzKpfw IIs – which were of diminishing utility on the 1942 battlefield – and PzBfWgs were in especially short supply at the front.

Tank strength of German panzer divisions used in the Caucasus campaign at the start of Operation *Fall Blau*, June 28, 1942

Unit	Pz II	Pz III (short 50mm)	Pz III (long 50mm)	Pz IV (short 75mm)	Pz IV (long 75mm)	PzBfWg	Total
6th Pz Rgt/3 PD	25	66	40	21	12	1	165
4th Pz Rgt/13 PD	15	41	30	12		5	103
201st Pz Rgt/23 PD	27	50	34	17	10	--	138
Total	67	157	104	50	22	6	406

An SS-Wiking PzKpfw III up-gunned with the longer version of the 50mm. Wiking was configured as a motorized division during the Caucasus campaign, and had received a panzer battalion, the 5th, before *Fall Blau*. The battalion would be expanded to a panzer regiment when Wiking became an SS panzer division later in the war. (Nik Cornish at www.Stavka.photos)

Hitler's plan for the summer offensive, codenamed *Fall Blau* (Case Blue), called for Army Group South to shatter the Red Army forces to its front, and then divide into one force (Army Group A) that would drive into the Caucasus to seize the oil fields, while another (Army Group B) protected its flank by advancing along the Don River towards Stalingrad. Army Group A consisted of the First Panzer and Seventeenth Armies. Led by veteran panzer leader General Ewald von Kleist, the First Panzer Army included the 3rd, 13th, and 23rd Panzer and the 16th and SS-Wiking Motorized Divisions when it drove into the Caucasus. Each of the panzer divisions had three panzer battalions, and the two motorized divisions one panzer battalion apiece, giving von Kleist a total of 11. The Seventeenth Army consisted of infantry and mountain divisions.

The 3rd, 13th, and 23rd Panzer Divisions used in the advance towards the Caucasus – designated Operation *Edelweiss* – were experienced formations. The 3rd Panzer Division was one of the Wehrmacht's initial three formed in 1935, and had participated in the Polish and French campaigns. Under the command of future Field Marshall Walter Model during Operation *Barbarossa*, the 3rd raced across Belarus, south to encircle Soviet forces defending Kiev, and then took part in the Operation *Typhoon* assault on Moscow. In May 1942, the division helped repulse the Red Army's disastrous Kharkov offensive. The 13th Panzer Division had been initially organized as a motorized infantry formation and fought in the Polish and French campaigns. In late 1940, it was reorganized as the 13th Panzer Division during Hitler's expansion of the armored force, from ten to 20 panzer divisions, and during *Barbarossa* fought as part of Army Group South. The 23rd Panzer Division was a new formation, formed in September 1941 and initially trained with captured tanks in France. Shipped to the Eastern Front in early 1942, the division received its baptism of fire during the defeat of the Soviet Kharkov offensive in May, before participating in the opening stages of *Fall Blau*.

The 16th and SS-Wiking Motorized Divisions attacked into the Caucasus along with the panzers. Motorized divisions, redesignated panzer grenadier divisions during 1942, consisted of six truck-born infantry and one panzer

The Seventeenth and First Panzer Armies each had two StuG III assault gun battalions during the Caucasus campaign. The StuG initially carried a short 75mm howitzer for direct fire support of the infantry, but in 1942 began to be fielded with a longer 75mm gun, making it a potent tank killer. (Photo by Sobotta/ullstein bild via Getty Images)

battalion, along with motorized artillery, antitank, flak, reconnaissance, engineer, and other support elements similar to those in a panzer division. The 16th Motorized Division shared its origins with the 16th Panzer Division. After the battle for France the 16th Motorized was split, with some elements used to form the new 16th Panzer Division, while others were retained as the 16th Motorized Division. Like the other motorized divisions assigned to Army Group South, the 16th received a panzer battalion, the 116th, before the launch of *Fall Blau*. The SS-Wiking Division was formed after the fall

A

THE PzBfWg III AND THE PzKpfw III

1. PzBfWg III Ausf.H command vehicle, SS Motorized Division "Wiking" Headquarters. To allow divisional, regimental, and battalion commanders to operate close to the front line, the *Panzerwaffe* produced PzBfWg or *Panzerbefehlswagen* specialized command tank variants. This version, based on the PzKpfw III Ausf.H, has a dummy main gun and the turret welded into place, and only retains a machine gun for close defense. Mounting a dummy gun gave room for additional command personnel and communications equipment. A total of 175 Ausf.H command variants were fielded from November 1940 to January 1942. This PzBfWg has been painted in desert colors to operate in the arid Caucasian steppe. SS-Wiking fought on the Terek River, before being transferred to von Manstein to help hold an escape route open for the First Panzer Army in early 1943.

2. PzKpfw III Ausf.L, 201st Panzer Regiment, 23rd Panzer Division. A 23rd Panzer Division Pzkpfw III Ausf.L armed with the long-barrel 50mm KwK 39 L/60, summer 1942. Although not as effective as the up-gunned PzKpfw IV with its long 75mm, the L/60 50mms mounted on the III Ausf.J and L gave German tankers an improved capability to engage Soviet tanks in 1942. This crew has mounted track sections to the vulnerable hull front for additional protection. German panzers began the Caucasus campaign painted with the standard 1942 "*Dunkelgrau*" panzer grey, as seen on this vehicle. Fuel supply was a major challenge for the First Panzer Army as it drove hundreds of kilometers through the desert-like steppe towards its distant objectives, and this PzKpfw III carries additional fuel jerrycans on the turret and a fuel drum on the rear deck. The 23rd Panzer Division battled its way to the Terek River during the campaign and was transferred on November 24 to participate in Operation *Wintergewitter* (*Winter Storm*), von Manstein's attempt to relieve the encircled Sixth Army at Stalingrad.

1

2

of France in 1940. Wiking was intended to be manned by recruits from the Netherlands, Belgium, and the Nordic states, although its personnel were primarily ethnic Germans throughout the war. Wiking was heavily engaged during *Barbarossa* while operating with Army Group South, and was the first SS division to receive an armored element when the 5th Panzer Battalion arrived in June 1942.

The Seventeenth Army, an infantry formation, had two *Sturmgeschütz* (assault gun) battalions, each with a table of organization strength of 28 StuG IIIs. The First Panzer Army also controlled two assault gun battalions. Completing the Axis motorized component was the 1st Slovak Mobile (Fast) Division of about 10,000 troops, primarily motorized infantry with an armored element with a mix of Czech-produced LT-35, LT-38, and LT-40 light tanks. Between the three panzer and three motorized divisions in Army Group A, the Wehrmacht was deploying a force of about 500 tanks to seize an area roughly the same size as France or Germany.

Panzer strength of motorized divisions used in the Caucasus campaign at the start of Operation *Fall Blau*, June 28, 1942

Panzer Battalion	Motorized Division	Pz II	Pz III (short 50mm)	Pz III (long 50mm	Pz IV (short 75mm)	Pz IV (long 75mm)	PzBfWg	Total
116th	16 Mot	10	–	35	–	8	1	54
5th	SS Wiking	12	12	24	4	–	1	53
Total		22	12	59	4	8	2	107

Soviet doctrine and organization

While the Wehrmacht's summer offensive was spearheaded by well-organized and experienced panzer and motorized divisions, the Soviet Union was struggling to rebuild, train, and reorganize its armored forces under the pressure of repeated defeats. After the huge losses of *Barbarossa*, the Red Army was reduced to supporting its rifle divisions with small tank brigades and separate tank battalions. During the winter counter-offensive, these brigades – often organized in ad hoc groups with cavalry or ski units – proved too small for effective deep penetrations of enemy defenses, and wasted away rapidly in combat. After the disappointments of the winter, the Soviet high command sought to improve its combat power by forming larger tank

T-26s of the 207th Tank Brigade, Transcaucasian Front, operating in December 1942 with infantry tank riders. Soviet tank units typically attacked with infantry aboard, leading to heavy losses to German artillery, mortar, and small arms fire. (From the fonds of the RGAKFD in Krasnogorsk via Stavka)

and mechanized corps. In size, these were the rough equivalents of Western divisions, each with three-to-four tank or motorized rifle brigades. Soon organized in tank armies, the new corps were intended to launch powerful drives deep into enemy rear areas, as visualized in the Soviet pre-war deep battle doctrine. In 1942, due to the imperative to defeat the enemy's attempt to capture Stalingrad, all the new tank corps that Moscow sent south to meet the *Fall Blau* offensive were committed against Army Group B.

In addition to the tank and mechanized corps, the Red Army retained large numbers of separate tank brigades, regiments, and battalions throughout the war to provide support to its rifle divisions. The January 1942 tank brigade's table of organization strength totaled ten KV-1 heavy, 16 T-34 medium, and 20 T-60 light tanks, organized in two mixed tank battalions. Tank brigades intended to support cavalry units had 20 T-34s and 26 T-60s. By the start of *Fall Blau*, the Red Army had a total of 98 separate tank brigades, 22 of them opposing Army Group South, although shortages of tanks meant that few brigades operated close to their full table of organization.

The losses of the first months of *Barbarossa* led the Soviet high command to also organize independent tank battalions (OTB or *otdel'nyy tankovyy batal'on*). The initial table of organization contained seven T-34 and 20 T-60 light tanks, but these proved too weak to provide adequate support to the rifle divisions. A November 1941 revision resulted in an OTB strength of 36 tanks, including five KV-1s, 11 T-34s, and 20 T-60s. Units in the field usually had lower numbers and were often using light tanks or surviving pre-war T-26 or BT models. About 80 OTBs were in the Red Army force structure in July 1942.

The Red Army formations in the south initially contained 2,750 tanks (about 30 percent of the Red Army total), but suffered heavy losses during the failed offensive to retake Kharkov in May and during the early days of *Fall Blau*. Reinforcing Soviet tank armies and corps were sent to contest the German advance towards Voronezh and to strike Army Group B's left flank as it advanced towards Stalingrad, suffering disastrous losses during their

US M3 medium tanks loaded onto railcars in Iran for transport to the USSR. Red Army units fighting in the Caucasus relied heavily on Lend-Lease tanks delivered via the Persian Gulf supply route, due to threats to their lines of communications with the north. (AC)

counterattacks during the summer months. To the south, the Red Army's battered Southern Front retreated through Rostov-on-Don towards the Caucasus with fewer than 100 operational tanks. When Army Group A's advance into the region severed the Tikhoretsk–Stalingrad line, the Soviets were only able to reinforce the Caucasus by shipments across the Caspian Sea.

Beginning in August, the defenders used newly arrived Valentines, Stuarts, and Lees arriving from the Persian Gulf Lend-Lease resupply route, along with smaller numbers of available Soviet-produced tanks to rebuild their brigades and independent battalions. By October, the Red Army's tank force in the Caucasus consisted of five tank brigades and four OTBs, totaling 313 tanks with seven KV-1s and 64 T-34s, and about 125 Lend-Lease types. After the late November Operation *Uranus* attack against Army Group B that encircled the German Sixth Army in Stalingrad, Soviet forces in the Caucasus joined in the counter-offensive. The Red Army in the Caucasus was now equipped with about 1,000 tanks but had no tank corps or armies. To improve its combat power, Soviet commanders hastily formed two ad hoc tank formations in early 1943, Tank Group Lobanov with 106 tanks and Tank Group Filippov with 123. The groups had about one third T-34s, with the rest light T-60s and Lend-Lease tanks.

TECHNICAL FACTORS

German tanks and AFVs

In 1942, the Wehrmacht's tank force was transitioning from its *Blitzkrieg*-era focus on mobility and reliability to heavier armor and long-range firepower. During the 1930s the German high command planned for a panzer force made up of PzKpfw III mediums with a 37mm gun capable of defeating enemy tanks, backed up by a smaller number of PzKpfw IVs to deal with enemy soft targets with its short-barreled 75mm. Production delays, especially with the critical PzKpfw III, led to the fielding of an interim light tank, the PzKpfw II, carrying a 20mm gun. During the campaigns of 1939 and 1940, the panzer divisions were forced to rely on large numbers of light tanks, including PzKpfw Is, a small, two-man machine-gun-armed tank intended for training, PzKpfw IIs, and (in 1940–41) Czechoslovakian-designed 35(t)s and 38(t)s. By June 1941, the majority of the panzer force was at last equipped with PzKpfw IIIs and IVs, although significant numbers of PzKpfw IIs and Czech-designed light tanks continued to be used in the main battle tank role.

A profile image of a PzKpfw III tank, up-gunned with a long 50mm main armament. Encounters with the well-protected T-34s and KV-1s in 1941 led to a rush to increase the firepower of German tanks, and the PzKpfw III Ausf.J and Ausf.L versions were fielded carrying the longer KwK 39 L/60 50mm gun. (Photo by Interim Archives/Getty Images)

Encounters with the Red Army's 76.2mm-armed KV-1 and T-34 tanks spurred the Wehrmacht to rapidly pursue armor and firepower upgrades. Most of the PzKpfw IIIs that invaded the USSR in 1941 carried the short-barreled KwK (*Kampfwagenkanone*) 38 L/42 50mm in place of the previous 37mm, but the inability of the L/42 to penetrate the frontal armor of the T-34 and KV-1 led

to a further upgrade using the KwK 39 L/60 50mm. The longer L/60 50mm improved capabilities against Soviet tanks, although about half of the PzKpfw IIIs used during the *Fall Blau* offensive still carried the shorter L/42 50mm gun. The PzKpfw IV was upgraded to carry the KwK 40 L/43, a long 75mm gun, giving it good capabilities against its Red Army opponents. The upgraded PzKpfw IVs only arrived in limited numbers in 1942 and the majority still carried the short 75mm during the Caucasus campaign. By the end of the year, the first small detachments of Tiger I heavy tanks equipped with the KwK 36 L/56 88mm arrived on the Eastern Front, highlighting the Wehrmacht's shift to more expensive, well-armored vehicles with highly-capable main guns, at some cost to reliability and mobility.

A PzKpfw IV advancing into action in the Caucasus, September 1942. The tank is an Ausf.F2 with a KwK 40 L/43, the first model mounting a long-barreled, high-velocity 75mm gun. The panzer commanders are advancing with their heads out of the hatch for improved battlefield situational awareness, a common German practice. (Photo by Arthur Grimm/ullstein bild via Getty Images)

Panzerkampfwagen III

The PzKpfw III was the main Wehrmacht battle tank in the early years of the war, although production shortfalls led to delays in the fielding of planned numbers in 1939–40. One of the major advantages of the PzKpfw III design was its five-man crew. With three crewmen in the turret, a dedicated loader and gunner loaded, aimed, and fired the main armament and coaxial machine gun, leaving the tank commander free to maintain situational awareness, designate targets, and direct the driver. The radio operator/hull machine gunner and the driver sat in the front of the hull. The PzKpfw III Ausf.E, the first mass-production model, had relatively light armor, good mobility, and carried a 37mm main gun along with hull- and turret-mounted machine guns.

A PzKpfw III carrying a fuel drum on its rear deck. The panzers often carried additional fuel during the long drive across the arid terrain north of the Caucasus Mountains due to problems resupplying the lead divisions. (Nik Cornish at www. Stavka.photos)

A German armored column on the move. The lead tank still carries a short 75mm main gun, useful for delivering high-explosive rounds against soft targets, but with limited effectiveness against the well-protected T-34s and KV-1s. The tank also carries tracks attached to the hull for additional protection. (Nik Cornish at www.Stavka.photos)

By 1941, German factories at last produced enough PzKpfw IIIs to allow this tank to assume its planned role as the primary gun-armed tank in the panzer divisions. Engagements in 1940 with heavier French and British tanks led to the development of the Ausf.F with the KwK 38 L/42 50mm gun. While an improvement over the 37mm, the L/42 was a short-barreled weapon and proved unable to penetrate the frontal armor of the T-34s and KV-1s encountered during the invasion of the USSR. Superior German training, experience, command and control, and crew ergonomics nevertheless allowed the panzers to prevail despite inadequate guns and armor. To meet the threat of improving enemy armor, the longer KwK 39 L/60 50mm was carried by some PzKpfw III Ausf.Js in early 1942, and equipped the subsequent L, K, and M models. The PzKpfw III's turret ring size was too small to mount a 75mm gun, leading to the up-gunned PzKpfw IV taking its place as the primary German battle tank in 1943. The PzKpfw III chassis continued to be used as the basis for the highly capable StuG III assault gun, soon converted to carry the long 75mm.

Panzerkampfwagen IV

The PzKpfw IV served as a support tank in the first years of the war, backing up the gun-armed PzKpfw IIIs with its short KwK 37 L/24 75mm main armament firing high-explosive rounds against enemy fortified positions, antitank guns, and pillboxes. Like the PzKpfw III, the IV had a five-man crew and coaxial and bow-mounted machine guns. The Wehrmacht planned to have the portion of IIIs to IVs in the force mirror the infantry's light-to-heavy machine-gun ratio, resulting in three PzKpfw IIIs for every IV. The short

B

STUG ASSAULT GUN AND PZKPFW IV

1. StuG III Ausf.F, 191st Assault Gun Battalion. By early 1943, the Seventeenth Army only had the low-strength 13th Panzer Division and two battalions of StuG III *Sturmgeschütz* assault guns for armored support. The Wehrmacht's assault gun units were manned by crews from the artillery rather than the panzer branch and were regarded as elite personnel. The StuG III Ausf.F carried the long-barreled 75mm, giving both an excellent high-explosive and armor-piercing capability. The StuG proved to be an extremely effective tank killer, with its low profile and good protection, and often destroyed its opponents from longer range and from ambush positions.

2. PzKpfw IV Ausf.F2, 13th Panzer Division. The *Panzerwaffe* began to field PzKpfw IVs carrying the long KwK 40 L/43 75mm gun in 1942, in response to the threat posed by the well-armed and well-protected T-34s and KVs encountered the year before. These were first placed on Ausf.F models, resulting in the Ausf.F2, followed by the Ausf.Gs. The longer 75mm allowed the PzKpfw IV to meet the T-34 on equal terms and changed what had been a support tank intended for engaging soft targets into the Wehrmacht's main battle tank. Unfortunately for the panzer divisions fighting on the Eastern Front and in North Africa, the up-gunned IVs only arrived in small numbers in 1942, and most PzKpfw IVs went into action with the older short 75mm "cigar butt" main gun. The 13th Panzer Division thrust south of Terek in November 1942, as part of the First Panzer Army's final effort to outflank and threaten Grozny, but was halted by fierce Red Army resistance. Ultimately, the division was encircled and had to break out, abandoning 80 tanks and over 1,000 motor vehicles.

1

2

Field maintenance on a PzKpfw IV Ausf.F2. The F2 was the first PzKpfw IV variant produced with a longer 75mm gun. The new KwK40 L/43 gave the tank the ability to fire a higher-velocity round able to penetrate the T-34's armor at normal combat ranges. The F2's main gun featured a rounded muzzle break, soon followed by a two-chambered one on the Ausf.G. (Nik Cornish at www.Stavka.photos)

75mm – dubbed the "cigar butt" by its crews – was effective against soft targets, but had minimal capabilities against the frontal armor of the T-34s and KV-1s encountered during *Barbarossa*.

To meet the threat posed by the T-34 and KV-1, Germany mounted the long 75mm KwK 40 L/43 on the most recent PzKpfw IV model, the Ausf.F. The Ausf. F2 was soon followed by the Ausf.G, and its long 75mm at last gave the panzer crews the ability to successfully engage the Soviet heavies and mediums from the front, in addition to side and rear. Reports from panzer units fighting during *Fall Blau* confirmed penetrating attacking T-34s at ranges up to 1,200m (circa 1,300yd). With 80mm of frontal armor protection, the PzKpfw IV proved capable of resisting fire received from the 76.2mm on the T-34 and KV-1, and the 75mm on the US M3. Unfortunately for the panzer divisions, the up-gunned PzKpfw IVs only arrived at the front in small numbers. The nine panzer divisions assigned to Army Group South for *Fall Blau* had a total of 135 PzKpfw IV lang ("long," for the long 75mm) on June 28, and the 11 armored battalions that advanced into the Caucasus with Army Group A contained only 30 PzKpfw IVs in late July.

Light tanks

Germany still had 860 PzKpfw IIs in its inventory in April 1942, although they were clearly too under-gunned and lightly armored to continue to serve as a main battle tank. As a result, the PzKpfw II was shifted towards a reconnaissance role, and the table of organization called for a five-PzKpfw II

C

AXIS LIGHT TANKS

1. LT-40 Light Tank, 1st Slovak Mobile (Fast) Division. Like other Axis allies, Slovakia sent troops to join Hitler's Operation *Barbarossa* invasion of the USSR in 1941. In 1942, the Slovakian Expeditionary Force was reorganized into the 1st Mobile and 2nd Security Divisions. The 1st Division primarily consisted of truck-mounted infantry supported by Czech-produced tanks, including the LT-35, LT-38, and LT-40. All were mobile, lightly armored, and carried a 37mm main gun. Slovakia had difficulty obtaining adequate numbers of LT-35s and LT-38s from Germany, but secured 21 LT-40s – a lighter version of the LT-38 – originally ordered by Lithuania but undelivered after it was occupied by the USSR in 1940. The LT-40 used the same chassis as the LT-38 but had a smaller turret and three- rather than four-man crew. The Slovakian division performed well during the offensive into the Caucasus, but lost heavily during the early 1943 retreat, and was soon withdrawn to the Crimea. The tank shown carries the national colors of Slovakia on the turret.

2. PzKpfw II Ausf.F, Headquarters 6th Panzer Regiment, 3rd Panzer Division. One of the PzKpfw IIs of the reconnaissance platoon of the panzer regimental headquarters, 3rd Panzer Division. The PzKpfw II was an interim tank design, but due to delays in the production of the PzKpfw III served in the main battle tank role during the first years of the war, before being assigned to reconnaissance platoons in 1942. Along with a coaxial machine gun, the tank carried a 20mm KwK 30 L/55 autocannon that fired ten-round clips. The tank retains the standard panzer gray *Dunkelgrau* paint scheme. Along with the 23rd, the 3rd Panzer Division attacked towards Grozny during the late summer and fall, battling to secure a crossing over the Terek River. After the Soviet victory at Stalingrad, the 3rd retreated with the First Panzer Army, escaping through Rostov, and ultimately operating in 1943 as part of Army Group South.

1

2

platoon for each PzKpfw III or IV panzer company. The PzKpfw II had a three-man crew – commander/gunner, loader/radio operator, and driver – and mounted a 20mm KwK 30 L/55 main armament with a coaxial 7.62mm machine gun in the turret. The PzKpfw II typically carried 180 rounds of 20mm ammunition, and the gun used ten-round magazines and had a high rate of fire. The PzKpfw II was able to successfully engage the Red Army's pre-war T-26s and BTs and T-60 and T-70 light tanks, although its armor was only proof against enemy small arms and remained vulnerable to the Red Army's 45mm antitank gun. There was a shortage of PzKpfw IIs at the front in 1942, and the First Panzer Army's three panzer divisions had only a total of 67, although they were authorized 74 each.

During the early years of the war, the Germans also made heavy use of Czechoslovakian-designed LT-35 and LT-38 light tanks, designated 35(t) and 38(t) in Wehrmacht service, after seizing the inventory and production facilities in 1939. The (t) stood for *tschechisch*, German for "Czech." The earlier LT-35 had a four-man crew, with two in the turret, and carried a 37mm gun, along with coaxial and bow machine guns. The several hundred 35(t)s available for *Barbarossa* were used to equip the 6th Panzer Division, but most were lost in combat or due to breakdowns during the final winter assault on Moscow. The more modern and reliable 38(t) had the same crew arrangement and armament, but was fast and rugged, and, unlike the 35(t), the Germans kept the tank in production. Both were excellent 1930s designs and performed well in France, but could no longer be used as a main battle tank after the panzer divisions encountered the T-34s and KV-1s in 1941. Only the 22nd Panzer Division fighting in the Crimea was initially equipped with the 38(t) in 1942, although LT-35s and LT-38s were used to equip several Axis allied mechanized units, including the Slovak 1st Mobile Division that operated as part of the First Panzer Army during the Caucasus campaign.

The new breed: *Panzerkampfwagen* VI Tiger I

In addition to mounting larger guns on its existing PzKpfw IIIs and IVs, the Wehrmacht planned to regain dominance in the tank-against-tank realm by fielding a superior medium tank, the PzKpfw V Panther. The Panther was still in the design and development phase in 1942 and would only be fielded in mid-1943 for the Operation *Zitadelle* offensive against the Kursk salient. As early as 1937, however, the German high command had been interested in

A PzKpfw II in the Caucasus, summer 1942. The PzKpfw II, produced as an interim design due to delays in the production of Pz IIIs and IVs, remained in the panzer division table of organization in 1942 as a reconnaissance vehicle. (Nik Cornish at www.Stavka.photos)

fielding a heavy "breakthrough" tank, and the effort accelerated in 1940–41 as the *Panzerwaffe* encountered heavily armored French, British, and Soviet tanks. Ultimately, a conventional Henschel design was selected to serve in the heavy tank role.

The resulting PzKpfw VI Tiger I's 100mm frontal armor and excellent 88mm gun gave it protection and firepower superior to any other 1942 tank. The Tiger was heavy, however, at 55–56 tons, had reliability problems, and was expensive and complex to produce. With only a small number available late in 1942, the Germans decided to dispatch small Tiger detachments to various fronts. Tiger companies were sent to Tunisia, the Leningrad area, and to reinforce Army Group B, which at the time was attempting to relieve the Stalingrad pocket. Arriving too late for the drive to reach the encircled Sixth Army, the Tigers of the 503rd Heavy Tank Battalion instead participated in the defense of Rostov-on-Don and subsequent defensive and counter-offensive operations in the Donbas region in early 1943.

Slovakian armor, including an LT-40 in the foreground and LT-35 to the rear. The Slovak 1st (Mobile) Division operating with Army Group A in the Caucasus in 1942 included a mix of LT-38s and LT-40s. The Slovaks had difficulties securing tanks from the German-controlled former Czechoslovakian armaments industry, but ultimately obtained 21 LT-40s – a scaled-down version of the LT-38 ordered by Lithuania but not delivered after the Soviet occupation in 1940. (Nik Cornish at www.Stavka.photos)

Sturmgeschütz **and** ***Panzerjäger***

The Germans had fielded modest numbers of *Sturmgeschütz* (assault gun) IIIs early in the war, with a short-barreled 75mm gun similar to that carried on the early PzKpfw IV on a turretless PzKpfw III chassis. StuG IIIs were manned by the artillery branch and used in an infantry support role. Due to the T-34 and KV-1 threat, a new version was introduced in 1942 with the long-barreled 75mm. The StuG had a low profile and 30–50mm of armor and proved to be effective both in infantry support and antitank roles.

German mechanized divisions contained a PaK (*Panzerabwehrkanone* – antitank gun) battalion operating both towed guns and mobile *Panzerjäger* (tank hunter) Marder IIs. The Marders mounted either captured Soviet 76.2mm or German 75mm PaK 40 guns on a modified PzKpfw II chassis.

A Tiger I tank in the USSR, 1942. With only a small number of Tigers produced, detachments were dispatched to Tunisia, the Leningrad area, and the southern USSR. Unfortunately for the Germans, an intact Tiger was captured near Leningrad and its capabilities analyzed by Soviet experts. (Photo12/ Universal Images Group via Getty Images)

A crew on their Marder II, a lightly armored *Panzerjäger* (tank hunter). The Marder II mounted either a captured Soviet 76.2mm gun or 75mm PaK 40/2 L/46, mounted on a modified PzKpfw II chassis. The Marder was part of the German effort to rush more-capable guns to the front after the shock of meeting T-34s and KV-1s in 1941. (Nik Cornish at www.Stavka.photos)

The vehicle had minimal armor protection and was open-topped, making it vulnerable to artillery or mortar fire or close infantry assault, but improved the antitank firepower available on the front line.

PzBfWg *(Panzerbefehlswagen)* command tanks

The Wehrmacht wanted panzer commanders to lead from the front and developed a series of tanks modified to carry commanders and additional radio equipment. The earliest variant, the Sd.Kfz. 265 *Panzerbefehlswagen*, was a heavily modified PzKpfw I chassis with a box-like superstructure and single machine gun, but it was too weakly protected and, by 1942, was replaced with command tanks based on the PzKpfw III. Versions of the PzKpfw III D, E, and H were all converted to *Befehlswagen* configurations, with the main gun replaced by a dummy weapon to allow room for more communications equipment in the turret, and a "bedstand" radio antenna over the rear deck of the tank.

Comparative technical characteristics of select tanks

	PzKpfw III Ausf.J	PzKpfw IV Ausf.F2	T-34	M3S Lee
Crew	5	5	4	7
Dimensions: L x W x H (m)	6.28 x 2.95 x 2.5	7.02 x 2.88 x 2.68	5.92 x 3.0 x 2.4	5.64 x 2.72 x 3.12
Loaded weight (tonnes)	21.5	25	29.1	28.1
Main gun	50mm KwK 39	75mm KwK 40	76.2mm F-34	75mm M2 or M3*
Main gun ammo	84	87	77	46
Engine (hp)	300	300	500	350
Max speed (km/h)	40	38	55	39
Range (km)	155	210	300	193
Upper hull front armor (mm)**	50mm at 9°, 50.6mm effective	80mm at 8°, 80.8mm effective	45mm at 60°, 90mm effective	51mm at 30°, 58.9mm effective
Total number produced (all tank variants)	5,774	8,553	84,070 (includes both T-34-76 and -T-34-85)	6,258

*In addition to the 75mm mounted in a sponson, the M3 medium also carried an M5 or M6 37mm gun in a fully rotating turret. 178 rounds could be carried for the 37mm.

**Armor is the effective thickness in mm – actual thickness in mm at angle from vertical.

Soviet tanks and AFVs

Because of the huge losses to its armored force during Operation *Barbarossa* – over 20,000 tanks by December 1941 – the USSR concentrated on maximizing the production of existing designs to rebuild as rapidly as possible. After the evacuation of Soviet tank factories to the safety of the Ural Mountains, the main goal became the construction of as many T-34s as possible, and the only modifications of the basic design allowed were those that simplified production. Primitive working conditions, unskilled labor, and the pressure to produce the tanks led to an increase in production flaws, but the number of T-34s leaving the factories grew steadily, reaching 1,200 per month in 1942. Soviet factories also produced lesser numbers of KV-1 heavy along with T-60 and T-70 light tanks, the latter two added as simpler designs that could be constructed by automotive factories. In addition to the T-34 medium, KV-1 heavy, and T-60 light tanks in the force in early 1942, the Red Army also employed surviving T-26 infantry support and BT-5 and BT-7 fast cavalry support tanks, along with an increasing inventory of Lend-Lease tanks including the Matilda, Valentine, M3 Stuart, and M3 Lee.

T-26 and BT-7

Driven by Stalin's plans to industrialize and field a modern, mechanized army, by the end of the 1930s the USSR had produced and fielded more tanks than all other nations combined. The most common model was the T-26, with over 11,000 ultimately leaving the factories. Based on the British Vickers 6-ton tank, the T-26 was a capable 1930s design, with good mobility and a 45mm main gun. The T-26 only carried 13–15mm of armor, however, adequate against small arms but not larger weapons. After engagements with the Japanese in the Far East, later models carried improved 20mm armor at an 18-degree angle. The T-26 acquitted itself well during the Spanish Civil War and against Japanese forces at Khalkhin Gol, but was less impressive in the difficult conditions of the 1939–40 Winter War.

In parallel with the T-26s, the Red Army developed a series of BT (*Bystrokhodnyy tank*) fast cavalry tanks. The primary versions in the

A T-26 and crew south of Rostov during the summer of 1942. Despite the loss of thousands of T-26s in 1941, a number remained in the force a year later. During the Caucasus campaign, T-26s that had been in training units in the North Caucasus and Transcaucasus Military Districts were soon sent into combat. (From the fonds of the RGAKFD in Krasnogorsk via Stavka)

A BT-7 "fast tank." The BT-5s and 7s were effective designs of the 1930s. The BTs shared a common crew layout – with a commander-gunner, loader, and driver – and the same 45mm main gun and coaxial 7.62mm DT machine gun armament as the T-26, but were able to achieve much higher speeds, particularly on roads. (Courtesy of the Central Museum of the Armed Forces, Moscow via Stavka)

force in 1941 were the BT-5 and -7. Both carried the same 45mm as the T-26, but had a Christie suspension that gave a higher speed and better overall mobility. BTs could drive up to 72km/h (circa 45mph) on roads when they operated with their tracks removed. Like the T-26, the BTs proved capable in the conflicts in Spain and the Far East, but with their thin armor were vulnerable to enemy antitank weapons.

By 1941, both the T-26 and the BT fleets were worn out. Although technically a match for the PzKpfw IIs and Czechoslovakian-designed 35(t)s and 38(t)s that made up a significant portion of the invading panzer divisions, they were destroyed in huge numbers. Despite the loss of thousands of these types, modest numbers survived into 1942, especially in the Soviet Far East and in other interior military districts including those in the Caucasus region.

T-34 and KV-1

The T-34 design emerged from an effort to replace the T-26 infantry support, BT fast cavalry, and T-28 medium with a "universal" tank, and the first models left the factories in 1940. The T-34 was an excellent balance of firepower, mobility, and protection that outperformed any other tank in the world in 1941. The F-34 76.2mm main gun could penetrate the frontal armor of the most capable German tanks – the PzKpfw III and IV – and was able to deliver a powerful high-explosive round against enemy soft targets. The T-34 carried 45mm of well-sloped frontal armor, providing excellent protection against most Wehrmacht antitank guns, while the powerful V-12 500hp diesel engine, Christie suspension and wide tracks gave the T-34 superb mobility.

D

RED ARMY LIGHT AND MEDIUM TANKS

1. T-26, 207th Tank Brigade, Transcaucasus Front. Despite the huge losses to the Soviet T-26 light and BT-7 cavalry tank fleets in 1941, many serving in the USSR's interior military districts as training tanks entered front line service into 1942. T-26s from the Transcaucaus Military District were part of the Soviet force that invaded Iran in 1941, and the 207th Tank Brigade was formed there in April 1942. In November, the unit was sent north to oppose the final German offensive in the Ordzhonikidze area. T-26s were effective tanks in the 1930s and could still support infantry or engage light Axis tanks with their 45mm main gun, but were of little use as main battle tanks. Soviet tanks were painted 4BO "tank green," and for security reasons did not carry standard markings. Unit commanders could direct their tanks to have special markings applied for traffic control or identification purposes, often in geometric shapes such as the diamond seen here.

2. T-34, 151st Tank Brigade, Transcaucasus Front. This T-34, produced in 1942, is similar to the 1941 version but with a series of small changes aimed at making the production process cheaper, simpler, and faster. Many T-34s rushed from the factories were found to have production faults once they reached the battlefield. The T-34 remained technically dominant on the battlefield, although German leadership, crew experience, and superior tactics still gave the panzer divisions the edge over their Red Army counterparts. In addition, the Wehrmacht was able to increase its capabilities by fielding improved *Panzerjäger* and up-gunning its StuG IIIs and PzKpfw IIIs and IVs with larger guns.

1

2

T-34s operating in the Caucasus in 1943. Early T-34s had a large, forward-opening hatch, making it difficult for Soviet tank commanders to operate in combat as panzer commanders often did, with their heads outside the tank for improved situational awareness. (From the fonds of the RGAKFD in Krasnogorsk via Stavka)

Although the T-34 so impressed the *Panzerwaffe* in 1941 that there were calls for Germany to produce a copy for its own forces, poor Soviet leadership, crew training, and the T-34's inferior crew ergonomics compromised its battlefield effectiveness. The driver had poor visibility, and the T-34 lacked a turret basket, complicating the job of the loader as he struggled to avoid spent shell casings and unpack ammunition stored in the floor. With a two-man turret crew, the tank commander had to also serve as gunner, making it difficult to aim and fire while simultaneously maintaining battlefield awareness and directing the driver. The T-34 lacked a commander's cupola, forcing him to rely on a limited-view periscope for visibility. Early T-34s had a single, large forward-opening turret hatch, making it difficult for him to ride – as German tank commanders often did – with his head out of the hatch in combat. Due to the lack of radios in many Soviet tanks, platoon, company, and battalion commanders often had to communicate with hand or flag signals while standing in the turret. The situation was worsened by the constant heavy losses suffered by Red Army tank units, which led to a stream of hastily trained and inexperienced crews being fed into battle.

The KV-1 heavy tank also shocked its Wehrmacht opponents in 1941, with attacking KVs breaking through German lines, their 70–90mm of armor impervious to all German weapons except the 88mm gun and heavy artillery pieces. The KV-1 carried the same 76.2mm main gun as the T-34s, but its armor increased its weight to 45 tons compared to the T-34's fully loaded 29.1 tons, and the KV, powered by the same engine, was slower and less mobile. Reliability was poor, with transmission problems common. The KV-1 had a five-man crew, but due to poor design the tank commander had to also serve as the loader for the main gun, with the third turret crewman assigned to man a rear-firing machine gun. By 1942, the KV-1's utility was being questioned, as it carried the same main gun as the faster and more reliable T-34, could not keep up with the T-60s and T-34s in the tank brigades, and was too heavy to use the standard Soviet pontoon bridge.

T-60 and T-70 light tanks

In the 1930s, the Red Army augmented its T-26 infantry support and BT cavalry tanks with a series of smaller amphibious light tanks used for scouting. The Soviets had just begun to field the T-40, an amphibious

Side view of a later T-34 with the slightly larger and easier-to-manufacture hexagonal turret. Shortages of rubber led Soviet factories to produce numbers of T-34s with steel-rimmed wheels. The vibrations generated were so severe that most were fielded with the first and last road wheels rubber-rimmed and only the center three steel-rimmed. (From the fonds of the RGAKFD in Krasnogorsk via Stavka)

replacement for the T-38, as *Barbarossa* began. Less than 50 T-40s entered service before the Soviets decided they needed to shift to a more easily produced light tank that could be assembled by automotive factories. The resulting T-60 lacked an amphibious capability and carried a two-man crew and 20mm main armament along with a coaxial machine gun. Although faster than the KV-1 at 44km/h (circa 27mph), the light T-60 lacked the speed to keep up with the 50km/h (circa 31mph) plus T-34s they were intended to operate with. The lack of a radio reduced any utility of the T-60 for reconnaissance missions, but while totally outclassed on the battlefield, over 6,000 T-60s would be produced during the first years of the war. In 1942, an effort to upgrade the T-60 led to the T-70 light tank. The T-70 had a 45mm main armament, giving a better antitank capability, but retained the T-60's two-man crew, dramatically limiting its combat effectiveness. Due to continued heavy T-34 losses, both the T-60 and T-70 were integrated into Soviet tank brigades in battalion strength as late as 1943.

Lend-Lease tanks

With the German invasion, the Western Allies rapidly agreed to supply a wide variety of equipment to assist the USSR. By the end of the war, a total of 11,660 tanks were dispatched to the USSR, the equivalent of 13 percent of Soviet production. Supply convoys began to arrive at the Soviet Arctic ports of Murmansk and Archangelsk in August 1941, but the sea lanes were vulnerable to Luftwaffe and U-Boat attacks from bases in Norway. The Anglo-Soviet invasion of Iran the same month opened another route, and ultimately 27 percent of Lend-Lease weapons and materiel would transit via the Persian Gulf into the southern USSR. The Persian Corridor would prove especially vital to Red Army forces defending the Caucasus in the summer and fall of 1942.

A Valentine tank on a vehicle transporter. The Valentine's good armor and high reliability was well received in the Red Army. The major shortcoming was the Valentine's 2-pounder 40mm gun, which could not fire a useful high-explosive round. Later versions sent to the USSR carried the 57mm 6-pounder, which had both a superior armor penetration capability and the ability to fire high explosives against soft targets. (Nik Cornish at www. Stavka.photos)

A Valentine of the 151st Tank Brigade, Transcaucasus Front, February 1943. The brigade was attached to the 47th Army in early 1943 and contained 25 T-26s and 19 Valentines. Later, a portion of the 20 British A17 Tetrarch light tanks sent to the USSR were assigned to the 151st. This Valentine carries one of the unit-specific marking schemes often seen on Red Army tanks. (From the fonds of the RGAKFD in Krasnogorsk via Stavka)

An M3L Stuart in Red Army service. The US-designed light tank was intended to carry up to five .30cal Browning machine guns, including one in an antiaircraft mount on the turret, one each in a coaxial and a bow position, and two in side sponsons set to fire directly forward. Soviet crews, like their US and British counterparts, typically removed the sponson machine guns, which had little utility in action. The pictured tank has one of the hull machine guns removed although the other is still mounted. (Nik Cornish at www.Stavka.photos)

Red Army evaluators were often critical of Western Lend-Lease tanks, often comparing them unfavorably to the excellent T-34 design, rather than the inferior light tanks that made up a major portion of the Soviet tank force. The first convoys to the USSR delivered Matilda II heavy tanks, which played a significant role in the defense of Moscow in late 1941. Matildas equipped several of the brigades in the first Soviet tank and mechanized corps formed in 1942, but do not appear to have been used in the Caucasus. The Matilda's armor was considered the equal of the KV-1's by the Red Army, but the tank was criticized for its poor mobility in muddy or snowy conditions, as well as its 2-pounder 40mm gun, which was unable to deliver a useful high-explosive shell.

Valentine infantry tanks soon arrived and would be one of the two tanks – the other being the M-4 Sherman – requested in large numbers by the Red Army later in the war. The Red Army designated the Matilda the Mark II, and referred to all Valentines, irrespective of their British model designation, as Mark IIIs. The Valentine was designed to be a less expensive and easier-to-produce tank than the Matilda. It had a modest speed of 25km/h (circa 15.5mph), and, unusually for an early-war British tank, good reliability, with a simple suspension and transmission system. The Valentine carried up to 65mm of armor but was saddled with the same 2-pounder carried by the Matilda. The three-man tank was very cramped, and the two-man turret crew arrangement forced the commander to also serve as loader for the main gun. The Valentine would be the most-produced British design during the war, with over 8,000 built, including chassis used for other purposes. Later variants of the Valentine were upgraded to carry the 6-pounder 57mm main armament. Although considered obsolete by the Western Allies in 1943, Valentines carrying the 6-pounders were requested by the Soviets in such numbers that the Allies kept production lines operating to meet the Red Army's needs.

An M3S medium tank in Red Army service. Although the Soviets referred to the M3s it received as Grants, they were actually in the Lee configuration, retaining the small turret with a .30cal Browning light machine gun atop the fully rotating 37mm turret. (AC)

M3 Stuart light and M3 Lee medium tanks were the US-designed models shipped to the USSR in 1941–42. Both were highly reliable, and the Stuart with its four-man crew and 37mm main gun was clearly superior to the T-60 and T-70. The 37mm, unlike the British 2-pounder/40mm, could shoot both useful armor-piercing and high-explosive rounds. Soviet officers were critical of the Stuart's narrow, rubber-padded tracks, which could pose mobility problems in muddy or icy conditions, and its limited maximum operational range of 120km (circa 75 miles). The first several hundred Stuarts were shipped to the USSR through Murmansk, but with the heavy losses to the Arctic convoys, more use was soon made of the Persian Corridor. Stuarts began to arrive via Iran in September 1942, with a total of 298 arriving during the year. To differentiate the light Stuart from the M3 Lee medium, the Red Army designated it the M3L (*legkhiy* or light).

The M3 Lee, designated M3S (*sredniy* or medium), was considered an outmoded design by Red Army evaluators. The US's initial inability to mount a 75mm main gun in a fully rotating turret resulted in its placement in a hull-mounted sponson on the Lee, giving it a limited traverse, with a smaller rotating turret with a 37mm gun atop the tank. The M3Ss sent to the USSR were in the original US configuration, designated Lees by British forces, with a small commander's machine gun turret atop the 37mm turret, but were often called Grants by the Soviets. The M3S was reliable but Soviet officers considered its armor and firepower inferior to the T-34 and KV-1. Seven crewmen were needed to operate the tank, which was tall and difficult to place in an effective hull-down firing position due to the awkward placement of the 75mm.

The Caucasus also saw the use of the only 20 British-produced A17 Tetrarch light tanks sent to the USSR. The British had developed and fielded machine-gun-armed light tanks before the war, and the Vickers-Armstrong firm pursued a private venture to mount a 2-pounder – the same gun as carried by British cruiser and infantry tanks – on a new light tank design. The resulting Tetrarch had unusual features, including suspension and steering systems that powered and turned each of the tank's four large road wheels, allowing for sharp changes in direction without skid-steering.

Personnel of the 151st Tank Brigade of the Transcaucasus Front familiarize themselves with one of the 20 A17 Tetrarch tanks received as part of the Lend-Lease program in December 1942. The Tetrarchs were used in combat the next year. (From the fonds of the RGAKFD in Krasnogorsk via Stavka)

The large road wheels themselves carried some armor. The British considered the tank obsolete early in the war, although small numbers were used in the 1942 invasion of Madagascar and eight were airlanded with the British 6th Airborne Division at Normandy. In response to the Red Army's urgent need for tanks during early 1942, 20 Tetrarchs were taken from the British 1st Armoured Division in the United Kingdom and sent via Iran to the Soviet Union. The tanks were attached to the 151st Tank Brigade and during training were featured in a number of photos taken for propaganda purposes.

THE CAMPAIGN

Hitler's drive for oil, July–November 1942

The offensive began on June 28 with Army Group South striking towards Voronezh, soon followed by attacks towards Rostov. Although Red Army forces avoided a major encirclement, they took heavy losses and were driven steadily back. Large numbers of Soviet tanks were lost in a series of hastily ordered counterattacks by the newly formed tank armies and corps against the German left flank at Voronezh, and along the Don River. With the initial phase of the offensive completed, Army Group South began its planned reorganization into Army Groups A and B. Army Group B's forces continued their advance, aiming to anchor the German left flank defenses by seizing Stalingrad on the Volga. In late July 1942, Army Group A captured Rostov, the gateway to the Caucasus, and began to launch its drive to the southeast.

The objectives for the operation, designated *Edelweiss*, were ambitious. The Soviet Maikop, Grozny, and Baku oil fields were 290km (180 miles), 650km (400 miles), and 1,100km (685 miles) distant, respectively, making logistical support a major challenge. German forces would have to deal with a poor road- and rail-net as well as difficult terrain, with the belt of farmland near Rostov soon giving way to desert-like steppe, followed by foothills and then the Caucasus Mountains themselves. German forces would have to secure crossings over the Don River at the beginning of the offensive, and

Panzers crossing the Don River south of Rostov, summer 1942, and beginning the Operation *Edelweiss* drive towards Maikop, Grozny, and Baku. (Photo by Heinrich Hoffmann/Mondadori via Getty Images)

would encounter a series of additional water obstacles as they drove deeper into the Caucasus region.

The Soviet defenders would need all the aid that terrain and distance could lend, given their losses during the disastrous Kharkov offensive in May, and during the first stages of *Fall Blau*. The primary Red Army formation defending the Rostov area, the Southern Front under General Rodin Malinovsky, attempted to establish a defensive line on the Don River, just to the south of the city, but only had four shattered armies with 112,000 troops and 17 operational tanks to defend a 155km (96-mile) front. The military districts to the south behind the front line, the North Caucasus and Transcaucasus, were lower-readiness commands that had been focused on mobilizing reinforcements for the front.

Field Marshall Wilhelm List's Army Group A, commanding the Seventeenth and von Kleist's First Panzer Armies, launched the *Edelweiss* offensive towards the Caucasus after securing Rostov on July 24. List planned to encircle Malinovsky's troops with a series of panzer-led thrusts across the Don River, and assisted by Brandenburger special forces teams, his divisions soon established bridgeheads and began to drive south. The 3rd Panzer Division was able to dash 40km (25 miles) beyond its crossing site and seized a new bridgehead over the Sal River, in the process defeating a Soviet counterattack led by a small number of T-60 light tanks. In a harbinger of future problems, the 23rd Panzer Division crossed the Don but ran out of fuel and had to wait for Luftwaffe Ju 52s to fly in before it could join the 3rd in the advance south.

The Red Army launched a major counterattack on July 28, leading to one of the few large tank-versus-tank engagements during the early phase of the campaign. The 135th and 155th Tank Brigades, newly arrived from Moscow, detrained and made a 50km (30-mile) road march to join with the 110th and 115th Cavalry Divisions for an attack against the flank of the German advance. The two brigades

A PzKpfw IV fords a water obstacle next to a damaged bridge, Caucasus front, summer 1942. In addition to long distances, arid desert-like terrain, foothills and mountains, the advancing panzer divisions faced a series of water obstacles including the Don, Manych, and Terek rivers. (Nik Cornish at www.Stavka.photos)

A StuG III assault gun crew loading ammunition. Loading, fueling, and maintaining vehicles were additional burdens faced by crews, exhausted by action and long road marches during the day. Logistics in the Caucasus were a challenge for Army Group A as it drove south through the arid terrain, with fuel shortages often halting the panzer divisions in their tracks until Luftwaffe Ju 52s could fly in additional supplies. (Nik Cornish at www.Stavka.photos)

totaled 40 T-34s and 40 T-70s but had no combat experience, and the hastily formed cavalry-mechanized formation lacked time for reconnaissance. The Soviet force advanced towards Martynovka and occupied the town on July 28, with elements of the 135th Tank Brigade and two cavalry regiments posted to the south as a flank guard. Unlike the ad hoc Soviet force, the nearby 23rd Panzer Division was a cohesive and battle-tested combined-arms formation. Rather than await attack, the 23rd pinned the Soviets in place with a frontal holding attack on Martynovka by its *Kradschützen* motorcycle battalion while a *Kampfgruppe* built around two panzer battalions from its 201st Panzer Regiment attacked to the south. The panzer battlegroup soon destroyed the flank guard and thrust north on July 29, closing on the main body of the Red Army force in Martynovka from the rear. A close-quarters tank-versus-tank duel ensued in and around the town. By the end of the day, the Soviet force was destroyed, its commander killed, and 1,000 prisoners captured. The Germans claimed 77 Red Army tanks knocked out, at a cost of three of their own. Soviet post-war accounts admit the counterattack was defeated but claim that 60 German tanks were destroyed.

Despite the publication of Stalin's famous "Not a Step Back" General Order No. 227 on July 28, the Soviet high command permitted the outnumbered remnants of the Southern Front to retreat. With the Martynovka counterthrust defeated, Malinovsky could only order a transition to delaying actions as the bulk of the surviving Red Army forces retreated south to the Caucasus Mountain passes. Malinovsky's forces were able to avoid encirclement, but command and control began to disintegrate as the units withdrew with the panzers in close pursuit. Only on the left flank were Soviet forces, reinforced by the 17th Cavalry Corps and the Maikop Tank Brigade with 30 tanks from the North Caucasus Military District, able to conduct coherent delaying actions.

Marshall Semyon Budyonny, a crony of Stalin's from the Russian Civil War era and commander of the North Caucasus Military District, was soon placed in overall command of the defense of the Caucasus. Soviet forces lost heavily during the retreat, and on August 13, Budyonny reported that the four armies of the Southern Front had no more than 12,000 "bayonets" in total, and only 15 operational tanks, mostly light models. In early August, given the Southern Front's lack of tanks, 4,500 of its trained tank crewmen were ordered to the rear to form new units and the Soviet high command ordered that the Caucasus front would be the priority for Lend-Lease tanks arriving via Iran.

A German StuG III in Krasnodar, captured by Seventeenth Army forces on August 9, 1942. The Seventeenth was supported by two StuG III battalions. The pictured *Sturmgeschütz* mounts the short 75mm howitzer, intended to support infantry by engaging targets such as machine-gun nests and pillboxes with direct fire. (Nik Cornish at www.Stavka.photos)

Although the Caucasus oil fields were his primary strategic objective for 1942, Hitler weakened Army Group A as it began its drive south. The 22nd Panzer and the *Grossdeutschland* Motorized divisions, earmarked as reserves for List, were sent to reinforce Army Group B and Army Group Center, respectively. All but two of the Eleventh Army's divisions in the Crimea, a potential follow-up force for *Edelweiss*, were sent north to operate against Leningrad. The First Panzer Army was left with three panzer and two motorized divisions, along with four infantry divisions, to seize the far-flung oil fields.

Despite these diversions, Army Group A's panzer forces achieved *Blitzkrieg*-era rates of advance for several weeks. The panzer divisions drove almost 100km (62 miles) during the first two days of the month alone, often using their *Kradschützen* motorcycle battalion as an advance guard, closely followed by panzer and motorized infantry *Kampfgruppen*. The 3rd Panzer Division encountered rare resistance from the 11th NKVD division at the Manych River, but a dash by Wehrmacht armored fighting vehicles over the top of an exposed cofferdam with Luftwaffe cover outflanked the defenses. On August 10, the SS-Wiking, 13th Panzer and 16th Motorized Divisions captured *Edelweiss*'s first objective, Maikop. The Soviets destroyed the wellheads, storage, and refinery facilities there before retreating – the panzers had been able to navigate towards Maikop by steering towards the flames – preventing the Third

E

TANK CLASH AT MARTYNOVKA, JULY 28–29, 1942

Early in the campaign, newly appointed commander of the defense of the Caucasus, Marshall Semyon Budyonny ordered a counterattack against the left flank of the First Panzer Army as it thrust south of the Don River. The 135th and 155th Tank Brigades, newly arrived from the Moscow Military District with a total of 40 T-34s and 40 T-70s, were joined with two cavalry divisions into an improvised corps and occupied the town of Martynovka on July 28. The nearby 23rd Panzer Division soon took the initiative, however, launching *Kampfgruppe Burmeister* with elements of the 201st Panzer Regiment and two motorized battalions against the Soviet's southern flank. The panzers scattered a flank guard of two cavalry regiments and tanks of the 135th Brigade south of Martynovka on the 28th, and the next day advanced north to attack the bulk of the Soviet force from the rear. Here, one of the 201st's PzKpfw IV Ausf.Gs fires at a burning T-34 which was trying to withdraw from the town. Another Soviet tank, a T-70, burns behind the T-34. The KwK 40 L/43 75mm on the up-gunned Ausf.F2s and Gs at last gave the panzers the ability to reliably destroy the well-protected Soviet tanks from the front. The first German tank company to thrust into Martynovka alone destroyed 12 T-34s, six T-70s, as well as three antitank and two infantry guns. The Soviet force was destroyed, with its commander killed, and 77 tanks destroyed or captured. The 201st Panzer Regiment lost three tanks, hit from the rear during the fighting in Marynovka.

A panzer column drives across the steppe towards the Caucasus Mountains. German mechanized forces raised clouds of choking dust as they drove through the desert-like terrain south of the Don and north of the mountain foothills in July and August 1942. (Nik Cornish at www.Stavka.photos)

Reich from obtaining the oil supplies. Simultaneously, the Seventeenth Army, composed of infantry and mountain troops supported by its two StuG III-equipped assault gun battalions, moved to the southwest to capture the Taman peninsula and secure the Black Sea coast. Soviet forces made a stand to defend Novorossiysk, the Black Sea Fleet's last major port. Major Peter I. Reshetin's 126th OTB lost 30 of its 36 T-26s supporting the defenders of the port's outer perimeter, buying enough time for the defenses to be built up.

After taking Maikop, List divided his forces, sending his mobile units against a variety of scattered objectives rather than concentrating his panzers to attack the oil fields of Grozny and Baku. The 13th Panzer, SS-Wiking and 16th Motorized divisions were sent to the southwest to seize the Caucasus Mountain passes leading to the Black Sea port of Tuapse. Despite initial progress, the panzers and follow-on infantry and mountain formations could not break through, and the port was never captured. On August 21, a detachment of the 1st Mountain Division raised the swastika flag atop Mount Elbrus, the highest peak in Europe, but German forces remained stymied along the line of the Caucasus for the rest of the campaign.

At the same time, List dispatched von Kleist's First Panzer Army with the remaining panzer divisions to cross the Terek River, take Groznyy, and ultimately advance through the eastern Caucasus and capture Baku. Von Kleist only had the 3rd and 23rd Panzer Divisions to lead this drive, and supply shortages, the need to deal with bypassed Soviet units, and increasing Red Army resistance to their front slowed the advance. Most of the available Luftwaffe aircraft had been pulled north to support the battle for Stalingrad,

F

US LEND-LEASE TANKS

1. M3L Stuart, 563rd Tank Battalion. Stuart M3Ls operated with Red Army tank forces in the Caucasus throughout the campaign. In February 1943, as part of their effort to drive the Seventeenth Army from its defensive positions in the Kuban Bridgehead, the Soviets launched an amphibious operation at Ozerekya Bay near Novorossiysk. The landing force included 30 Stuarts of the 563rd Tank Battalion, but heavy German fire repulsed the landing. A secondary beach assault, however, was able to dig in and hold a small bridgehead dubbed the "Little Land" and held for months until the German withdrawal in September 1943. The Stuart depicted, like most US Lend-Lease tanks, were left in their original olive drab paint by the Red Army.

2. M3S Lee Tank (unknown unit), summer 1942. The Red Army was unenthusiastic about the M3 Lee medium tanks – designated M3S (*Sredniy*) to differentiate them from the M3L Stuart lights – that it received in 1942. The Lee's main 75mm was mounted in a sponson on the tank's right side, allowing only a limited traverse and making it difficult to position the tank in hull-down positions. Most tellingly, the tank had a high profile, increasing its battlefield vulnerability. This M3S was photographed in a Caucasian village after being captured by the 23rd Panzer Division, and its original US identification number is still visible. The German markings on the turret indicate the date captured, and on front of the tank there are shipping instructions to transport the M3S to Germany for technical evaluation. This M3 carries the longer M3 75mm, but due to shortages some carried the shorter M2, requiring the addition of a compensating weight to the end of the M2 barrel to allow the stabilizer, designed for the longer M3, to function.

1

2

German propaganda asserted that Army Group A had entered Asia when it crossed the Manych River in August. Here, tank crewmen meet a Tatar tribesman in the arid terrain north of the Caucasus Mountains. (Photo by Arthur Grimm/ullstein bild via Getty Images)

leaving von Kleist's divisions vulnerable to attacks by Soviet Pe-2 and A-20 bombers, and the Red Army flew six airborne brigades to strengthen their defenses on the Terek River. By August 23, the panzer divisions were able to reach Mozdok, destroying two Red Army armored trains, and securing the town two days later. The 23rd Panzer Division commander, General Erwin Mack, was killed on August 26 by artillery fire during the operation.

Von Kleist's forces now prepared to attack cross the Terek River, the last barrier before Grozny. Soviet forces in the area included the 52nd Tank Brigade and the 249th, 258th, and 563rd Separate Tank Battalions with a total of 195 tanks. The OTBs consisted largely of US and British Lend-Lease types. On August 23, two battalions from the 3rd Panzer Division were able to get across the river, but could not expand the bridgehead. Three days later, elements of the 111th Infantry Division secured a better crossing site and were soon reinforced by two panzer companies from the 23rd Panzer Division. The 249th OTB counterattacked with 25 T-34s along with the 62nd Naval Infantry Brigade but lost seven tanks to the Germans. The Soviets committed additional armor – up to 60 tanks in one attack – while von Kleist's forces struggled to reinforce the bridgehead. Kleist committed the 13th Panzer Division across the Terek on September 13th, allowing for several weeks of grinding progress. The SS-Wiking Division had been released from the Tuapse axis and soon joined the attempt to expand the Terek bridgehead. On September 28, the SS troops met a counterattack by two Soviet tank brigades, resulting in close-range engagements at 200–400m. The Wiking troops reported the loss of 12 tanks and claimed to have knocked out 11 Soviet counterparts. In early October, German forces, completely spent, shifted to a defensive posture on the Terek.

Frustrated with the lack of progress towards the oil fields, on September 10, Hitler relieved List and assumed direct command of Army Group A, resulting in Kleist serving as the de facto army group commander, in addition to his role leading his First Panzer Army. Kleist ordered his forces to prepare defensive positions for the winter after the Terek offensive ground to a halt, but in October the Germans identified a weak point in the Soviet defenses, which led to a renewed attack aimed at seizing the city of Ordzhonikidze. Taking the city would halt the arrival of Soviet reinforcements from the Georgian SSR (Socialist Republic) and could potentially open the way for a renewed push against Grozny.

The attack started well, with the Luftwaffe striking the 37th Army's headquarters and the 13th and 23rd Panzer Divisions again able to advance south. A series of engagements with Red Army tank brigades ensued, with the 13th Panzer engaging in an intense battle with the 52nd Tank Brigade on October 31. After nearing Ordzhonikidze, the advance bogged down as Soviet reinforcements, including the 5th Guards and 2nd Tank Brigades,

Troops of the 1st Mountain Division with armored support, summer 1942. During August, Army Group A commander Field Marshall Wilhelm List diverted the 13th Panzer Division and the SS-Wiking and 16th Motorized Divisions to the southwest, to assist the Seventeenth Army's attack through the Caucasus passes towards the Black Sea port of Tuapse, reducing the number of mechanized divisions available to advance on the Grozny oil fields. (Nik Cornish at www.Stavka.photos)

blocked the panzer divisions. The 13th Panzer was ultimately encircled but escaped the Red Army ring, abandoning 80 tanks and 1,088 trucks. A brief calm settled over the Caucasus front in late November. The heavy fighting had steadily worn down the panzer divisions, and Kleist had fewer than 150 operational tanks in December.

Tank strength of German panzer divisions, Caucasus campaign, November 18, 1942

Unit	Pz II	Pz III (short 50mm)	Pz III (long 50mm)	Pz IV (short 74mm)	Pz IV (long 50mm)	PzBfWg	Total
6th Pz Rgt/3 PD	13	19	25	5	3	1	66
4th Pz Rgt/13 PD	4	7	14	1	3		29
201st Pz Rgt/23 PD	5	12	15	4	4		40
Total	22	38	54	10	10	1	135

Retreat from the Caucasus, December 1942 to January 1943

Both sides briefly transitioned to a defensive posture, but Army Group A's strategic position in the Caucasus was soon imperiled by developments to the north. On November 19, Soviet forces launched Operation *Uranus*, smashing the Romanian forces guarding the flanks of General Paulus's Sixth German Army in Stalingrad, and soon encircled it. Four days later, Kleist was ordered to send the 23rd Panzer Division north to participate in Operation *Wintergewitter* (*Winter Storm*), an attack to break through the Soviet encirclement to relieve Paulus' troops. Although the Red Army began to increase pressure on Kleist's weakened lines, Hitler was determined to retain his position in the Caucasus and refused to allow any retreat.

By late December, the failure of *Wintergewitter* made it clear that the Sixth Army was doomed. Worse, Red Army formations were closing on Rostov, threatening to cut off Army Group A, whose lead positions were hundreds of kilometers away on the Terek and in the Caucasus. SS-Wiking was ordered north to help the Axis forces trying to hold off the advance on Rostov, and Hitler, after Stalingrad briefly more concerned with the threat of another encirclement, allowed Kleist to begin preparations to withdraw.

Panzer grenadiers sheltering behind a 23rd Panzer Division tank as they attack towards the Caucasus in September 1942. By the late summer and early autumn, the First Panzer Army's offensive towards the Grozny oil fields bogged down on the Terek River. (Photo by Arthur Grimm/ullstein bild via Getty Images)

The Soviet forces in the Caucasus were now organized into two major groupings, the Northern Group in the Terek area and a Black Sea Group along the mountains and seacoast to the west. Each controlled four armies along with several tank brigades and OTBs. The Red Army now had over 1,000 tanks available in the Caucasus, with the bulk assigned to the Northern Group. For its 1943 offensive, as it still lacked any tank or mechanized corps, the Northern Grouping formed two ad hoc tank groups to improve its armored striking power. Group Lobanov initially contained 106 tanks, including 46 T-34s, 24 T-70s, 12 T-60s, 18 Valentines, and six Stuarts in its 2nd, 15th, and 63rd Tank Brigades and 225th Tank Regiment. The group lacked maintenance and supply elements, but included a trucked rifle brigade, antitank and antiaircraft regiments, and an armored car battalion. Group Filippov operated 123 tanks in its 52nd, 140th, and 207th Tank Brigades along with the 266th and 562nd OTBs, as well as a naval infantry brigade and two antitank regiments. The Black Sea Grouping received some tank reinforcements and operated a total of 226 operational tanks, 147 of them Lend-Lease types, when it launched its offensive in mid-January.

Black Sea grouping of forces' operational tank strength, mid-January 1943

Unit	Subordinate to	Operational Tanks
151st Tank Brigade	47th Army	44 (25 T-26, 19 Valentine)
62nd OTB	47th Army	29 (9 Valentine, 20 Stuart)
126th OTB	47th Army	22 (3 T-34, 2 BT-7, 8 T-26, 9 T-60)
563rd OTB	47th Army	30 (9 M4A2, 21 Stuart)
564th OTB	56th Army	30 (10 T-34, 20 Stuart)
258th OTB	56th Army	30 (9 Valentine 21 Stuart)
5th Guards Tank Brigade	56th Army	40 (6 M3 medium, 18 Valentine, 16 M3 Stuart)
Total		225 operational tanks

The First Panzer Army planned to withdraw from the Terek on January 2, but on New Year's Day, Soviet forces led by the Northern Group's Tank Group

A PzKpfw III leads a column of the SS-Wiking Division. On September 28, tanks of the 5th Panzer Battalion and other elements of the division attacking across the Terek at Sagopshi were counterattacked by two Soviet tank brigades. The engagement resulted in the loss of 11 Soviet and 12 German tanks, and the Wiking Division attack petered out in early October. (Nik Cornish at www.Stavka.photos)

Lobanov struck the 3rd Panzer Division's defenses, leading to an immediate German pullout from their forward positions. Although Lobanov's tanks were able to overrun a regiment of the 50th Infantry Division, the Northern Group advance was poorly organized, and the rest of Kleist's forces were able to break contact and successfully withdraw. To the west, the Black Sea Grouping had difficulty deploying its tanks in the constrained terrain and was largely confined to using platoon-sized tank units for infantry support.

The Red Army's advance continued, and with Soviet tanks nearing Rostov in late January, the situation became critical. Hitler wanted to retain a force in the Kuban region to maintain a threat to the oil fields in 1943 and originally ordered all of Army Group A to withdraw to the Kerch Straits. After some hesitation, he allowed Kleist to pull the bulk of the First Panzer Army back through Rostov, where it played a critical role in von Manstein's "backhand blow" counteroffensive that stabilized the front in the early spring. The Seventeenth Army, however, was ordered to retreat towards Kerch to secure a foothold in the Caucasus, soon known as the Kuban Bridgehead.

Stalemate in the Kuban, February–October 1943

The bridgehead had not been prepared for defense, and supply by sea and air over the Kerch Straits was difficult in the early weeks of 1943. Of the five mechanized divisions that had advanced into the Caucasus in 1942, only the 13th Panzer Division joined the retreat to the Kuban. The division had few tanks at this time, and the Seventeenth Army commander split the formation into several small battlegroups that were attached to support his separate infantry corps. By April, the 13th Panzer Division had 26 operational tanks, including one PzKpfw II, three PzKpfw IIIs with the shorter 50mm gun, and

A PzKpfw III with *Winterketten* attached to its tracks for improved mobility in winter conditions. The *Winterketten* snow tracks were wider and had ice cleats for better flotation and traction in snowy conditions. (Nik Cornish at www.Stavka.photos)

19 with the longer version, two PzKpfw IVs with the long 75mm, and one PzBef command tank. The 13th Panzer only received new tanks – 30 PzKpfw IVs with the long 75mm – in July, but the division was withdrawn from the Kuban the next month. The Seventeenth Army also retained its two assault gun battalions now with 15 StuG IIIs each, along with the 525th Anti-Tank Battalion which had two companies of mobile Marder II mobile *Panzerjäger* antitank guns along with a towed antitank gun company. The Slovak 1st Mobile Division was withdrawn to the Crimea in February, but in May, a Romanian battalion with Czech-designed 38(t) light tanks, designated T-38s by the Romanians, was sent to reinforce the Kuban.

Despite Hitler's interest in maintaining a threat to the Soviet oil fields, planning for the summer of 1943 focused on mounting a major offensive – Operation *Zitadelle* – against the Red Army-held Kursk salient to the north. The Soviet high command, forewarned of German intentions, began to build up massive defenses around Kursk, but were also determined to eliminate the Kuban bridgehead in early 1943. The attacking Transcaucasus and North Caucasus Fronts initially contained a total of four tank brigades, a tank regiment, and nine OTBs, which were distributed among the attacking rifle divisions for infantry support. The Soviets had about 275 tanks, but the number of T-34s was limited, and over half were Lend-Lease types, including 70 M3 Lee and 70 M3 Stuart tanks, along with 30 Valentines. The remainder of the inventory consisted of T-60s and T-26s. Red Army troops also pressed nine captured PzKpfw IIIs and four PzKpfw IVs into service.

Initially, the Soviet high command expected rapid progress when the attacks on the Seventeenth Army began in late January. When the offensive lagged, Stalin ordered an amphibious attack on the key port of Novorossiysk, hoping to unhinge the German right flank. Thirty M3L Stuarts from the 563rd OTB were to be landed with the main assault at Ozerekya Bay south of the city. Soviet coordination of the landing operation was poor, with bombardments by Black Sea Fleet ships alerting German defenses before the assault. Tanks, landing craft, and assaulting troops were shelled by German artillery overlooking the beach, and only 12 of the M3Ls reached the shore

with the naval infantrymen. Six of the Stuarts were able to exit the beach and overrun some enemy guns but were destroyed as they attempted to seize their objectives inland. The entire Ozerekya operation soon collapsed, but a small diversionary landing by the 305th Naval Infantry Battalion a few miles to the east was able to establish positions ashore. Using antitank rifles and effective small-arms fire, the naval infantrymen repulsed the first tentative counterattacks by StuG III assault guns and infantry platoons. The Soviets shifted follow-on troops intended for Ozerekya to reinforce the 305th and soon built up the bridgehead to a strength of 10,000 troops. The isolated position, known as the *Malaya Zemlya* (Little Land), was held until the final recapture of Novorossiysk in September.

A T-34 with both "Mickey Mouse" turret hatches open and crewmen and infantry aboard in the Caucasus, spring 1943. Soviet forces pursued the retreating Army Group A during the winter, but were unable to drive the Seventeenth Army from its defensive positions in the Kuban despite a series of costly offensives in 1943. (Courtesy of the Central Museum of the Armed Forces, Moscow via Stavka)

Although the amphibious operation had failed, the attacks by the two Soviet fronts were able to force the Seventeenth Army from its forward positions. Krasnodar was recaptured, and Axis forces withdrew to the much shorter lines by February 25. Soviet forces kept attacking in March, including an attack by two rifle divisions of the 9th Army supported by 40 M3 Lee Medium tanks from the 92nd Tank Brigade and 132nd OTB against the battered German 50th Infantry Division on the 26th. Attacking over waterlogged terrain, the tanks were hit by enemy artillery and antitank guns and lost heavily.

Soviet air and naval forces failed to effectively interdict Axis supply lines over the Kerch Straits, and with the amphibious operation frustrated, the Red Army launched a series of frontal attacks on the Axis defenses during April and May. The fighting resembled World War I trench warfare and

The Soviets attempted an amphibious landing south of the port of Novorossiysk in February 1943. The main landing, which included a battalion of 30 M3L Stuart light tanks, was repulsed, but a smaller, secondary landing force secured a small bridgehead known as the "Little Land," that held out until the city was finally captured in September. (Photo by Mondadori via Getty Images)

the attacking Soviet units suffered heavy tank and infantry losses. After the failure of the initial two offensives in April, the Soviet high command made efforts to strengthen the armored force attacking on the Kuban front. The OTBs were disbanded, and four new tank regiments sent as reinforcements. The regiments were 20–40 tanks strong, and two were equipped with T-34s, and one, the 6th Guards, with 21 KV-1s. Impressed with the effectiveness of the StuG III, the Red Army had begun to field its own self-propelled artillery regiments in 1943, and two were also sent, each with eight Su-76 and 12 Su-122s. The North Caucasus Front now had about 400 tanks, but due to the difficult terrain and lack of any tank corps for exploitation, had difficulties effectively massing its armored striking power.

G

BRITISH LEND-LEASE TANKS

1. Valentine Mk.III, 5th Guards Tank Brigade. A Valentine tank operating with the 5th Guards Tank Brigade, 1942. The tank retains its British color scheme, and has a series of turret markings, including the 5th Guards-specific white diamond rhomboid. The Valentine had 65mm of armor, giving it good protection, a low profile, and could advance at 25km/h (circa 15.5mph). Although an effective infantry support tank, the Valentine carried the British 2-pounder 40mm and lacked the ability to fire a useful high-explosive round. Valentines lacked a bow machine gun and carried a coaxial 7.62mm BESA or US .30cal Browning, with the latter equipping Valentines produced in Canada.

2. Tetrarch Light Tank, 151st Tank Brigade. The Soviets received 20 British A17 Tetrarch light tanks via Iran in late December 1941. The tank resulted from an initiative effort by Vickers designers to mount the 40mm 2-pounder – the standard early-war armament of cruiser and infantry tanks – on a light tank. Small numbers were produced for British forces, but the design was rapidly considered obsolete. The Red Army considered the Tetrarch to be the equivalent of their own 45mm-armed T-70 light tank, and used the 20 it received in combat in early 1943. Losses and maintenance issues, exacerbated by a lack of spare parts, reduced numbers to just two by the autumn of the year.

1

2

Assault gun crewmen at rest in front of their StuG III in the Kuban, August 1943. With their low silhouette and up-gunned with a long 75mm main gun, the StuG III proved to be an excellent tank killer while supporting the Seventeenth Army's defensive battles in the Kuban. (Photo by Mondadori via Getty Images)

On May 26, the Red Army was ready to launch its third major offensive against the Seventeenth Army. The primary thrust by the 56th Army massed infantry and artillery, supported by the 92nd and 151st Tank Brigades and 257th Tank Regiment with about 145 tanks in total. The offensive made initial progress, severely damaging the German 101st Light Division, but the 56th only had a single NKVD division as an exploitation force. By the evening of the first day, 116 Red Army tanks had been lost, many to German mines, and only 26 recovered for repair. Numbers of the surviving tanks withdrew to refuel and failed to reenter battle. Fighting continued for several days, and on the 31st the 13th Panzer Division counterattacked with a battlegroup with a panzer-grenadier battalion and 12 PzKpfw IVs. The 21 StuG III assault guns of the 191st Assault Gun Battalion joined in the counterattack but were unable to restore the original line. In mid-July, the Soviets launched their fourth major offensive, again an unimaginative frontal attack, and again made little progress. When the offensive was called off in early August, the Red Army had sustained over 160,000 casualties and the Seventeenth Army 22,000. Exhausted, both sides ceased offensive operations.

ANALYSIS

For the German panzers, the early weeks of Operation *Edelweiss* were a return to the glory days of earlier *Blitzkrieg* offensives, with their mechanized columns driving rapidly through shattered Red Army units. The First Panzer Army's battle-hardened panzer and motorized divisions, now with numbers of up-gunned PzKpfw IIIs and IVs, quickly dealt with the few outnumbered Soviet tanks they faced as they advanced south of the Don River.

Maikop was soon captured, but Hitler and List squandered any chance of seizing the Grozny or Baku oil fields by weakening and dispersing Army Group A's armored striking power. Despite Hitler's designation of the Caucasus oil fields as the major strategic objective for 1942, he became obsessed with the battle to capture Stalingrad, and diverted additional forces, supplies, and air support to reinforce the German Sixth Army's battle for the city. At the Army Group level, List split his small force of mechanized divisions after seizing Maikop, sending three towards the mountain passes to lead the way to Tuapse, leaving only two for the initial attack towards Grozny. Later, the 16th Motorized was diverted to Elitsa, 500km (310 miles) north of Grozny, to maintain a tenuous link with Army Group B rather than joining in the attack towards the oil fields. By October, Army Group A was finally halted on the Terek River and along the Caucasus Mountains by terrain, logistics, and growing Soviet resistance.

In engagements between German and Soviet tank units, the panzer units enjoyed qualitative advantages in experience, training, and tactical expertise, and

A T-34 enters the shattered city of Novorossiysk. On September 16, 1943, Soviet forces at last relieved the isolated "little land" bridgehead and recaptured the city; German forces completed their withdrawal from the Kuban to Crimea on October 9. (Courtesy of the Central Museum of the Armed Forces, Moscow via Stavka)

at the beginning of the campaign were in the unusual position of outnumbering their Red Army opponents. After defeating the Soviet counterattack at Manych, von Kleist's forces only encountered scattered Red Army tank formations for several weeks. By late August and early September, however, the Soviets regained their cohesion and established strong defensive lines in the Caucasus passes and on the Terek River. With its rebuilt tank brigades and battalions to support the defending rifle divisions, Red Army forces on the Terek River line were able to frustrate repeated attempts by the First Panzer Army to renew its advance. With Stalingrad the focus of Soviet efforts during the 1942 winter counter-offensive, there were no tank or mechanized corps available for the Caucasus, and when Army Group A began to withdraw, the Red Army was unable to prevent the First Panzer Army's escape through Rostov and the Seventeenth Army's move towards the Kerch Straits.

Armor played a less prominent role during the fighting for the Kuban bridgehead. The Seventeenth Army had a very limited armored force, although it made good use of its StuG III assault guns to strengthen its antitank firepower, and the weak 13th Panzer Division was available as a mobile counterattack force. The Red Army used its tank brigades, regiments, and OTBs in their intended infantry support role, but due to poor terrain, enemy resilience, and unimaginative tactics took heavy losses and made little progress.

Ultimately, Axis forces would evacuate to the Crimea – not because of Soviet attacks to their front, but due to the failure of *Zitadelle* and the subsequent successive Red Army offensives against Army Group South. The 13th Panzer Division departed in August, and, by September, the Seventeenth Army began to withdraw across the Kerch Straits to Crimea. The Soviets attempted to pressure the retreat but were unable to pin any German formations in place and the Luftwaffe repeatedly intervened to break up the attacking tank-infantry formations. The Axis was ultimately able to withdraw 227,000 troops to the Crimea. Any pretense of a renewed German threat to the Caucasus and its oil was over.

FURTHER READING

Robert A. Forczyk's Osprey Campaign Volumes, *The Caucasus 1942–1943: Kleist's race for oil* (Osprey, 2015) and *The Kuban 1943: The Wehrmacht's last stand in the Caucasus* (Osprey, 2019) provide excellent overviews of the 1942 and 1943 campaigns in the Caucasus. Andrei A. Grechko's, *Battle for the Caucasus*, (Military Publishing/Central Books,1967) and Wilhelm Teike's *The Caucasus and the Oil, The German-Soviet War in the Caucasus 1942/43* (J.J. Fedorowicz, 1995) provide more detailed accounts from the Soviet and German perspectives. Steven J. Zaloga's *Armored Champion: The Top Tanks of World War II*, (Stackpole Books, 2015) includes in-depth analysis of the key tanks of 1942, as well as an excellent framework for technical and tactical analysis of World War II tanks and armored fighting vehicles. Robert Forczyk's two books on armored warfare on the Eastern Front, *Tank Warfare on the Eastern Front, 1941–1942: Schwerpunkt*, (Pen & Sword Military, 2015) and *Tank Warfare on the Eastern Front, 1943–1945: Red Steamroller* (Pen & Sword Military, 2016) feature chapters with additional in-depth analysis of the 1942–43 armored struggle in the east.

The campaign

Forczyk, Robert A., *Kharkov 1942: The Wehrmacht strikes back* (Campaign 254), Osprey, Oxford (2013)

Glantz, David M., *Operation Don's Left Wing: The Trans-Caucasus Front's Pursuit of the First Panzer Army,* November 1942–February 1943, University of Kansas Press, Lawrence (2019)

Glantz, David M., *Stalingrad,* University of Kansas Press, Lawrence (2009)

Glantz, David M., *To the Gates of Stalingrad,* University of Kansas Press, Lawrence (2019)

Kirchubel, Robert, with Komar, Gary, *Atlas of the Eastern Front: 1941–45*, Osprey, Oxford (2016)

Vail Motter, T.H., *The United States Army in World War II: The Middle East Theater: The Persian Corridor and Aid to Russia,* Center of Military History, United States Army, Washington DC (2000)

Ziemke, Earl F., *Moscow to Stalingrad: Decision in the East*, Office of the Chief of Military History, United States Army, Washington DC (1987)

Ziemke, Earl F., *Stalingrad to Berlin: The German Defeat in the East*, Office of the Chief of Military History, United States Army, Washington DC (1968)

Soviet tanks and forces

Baryatinsky, Mikhail, *Light Tanks: T-27, T-38, BT, T-26, T-40, T-50, T-60, T-70*, Ian Allan Publishing, Hersham (2006)

Glantz, David M., *Colossus Reborn: The Red Army at War, 1941–1943*, University of Kansas Press, Lawrence (2005)

Glantz, David M., *Companion to Colossus Reborn: Key Documents and Statistics*, University of Kansas Press, Lawrence (2005)

Kinnear, James, and Pasholok, Yuri, *T-60 Small Tank & Variants,* Canfora, Stockholm (2017)

Klapdor, Ewald, *Viking Panzers: The German 5th SS Tank Regiment in the East in World War II*, Stackpole Books, Mechanicsburg PA (2011)

Samsonov, Peter, *Designing the T-34: Genesis of the Revolutionary Soviet Tank*, Gallantry Books, Horncastle (2019)

Samsonov, Peter, *Panzer III vs T-34: Eastern Front 1941* (Duel 136), Osprey, Oxford (2024)

Sharp, Charles S., *Volume II: School of Battle: Soviet Tank Corps and Tank Brigades January 1942 to 1945*, George F. Nafziger (1995)

Sharp, Charles S., *Volume III: Red Storm: Soviet Mechanized Corps and Guards Armored Units 1942 to 1945*, George F. Nafziger (1995)

Sharp, Charles S., *Volume XII: Red Hammers: Soviet Self-Propelled Artillery and Lend Lease Armor 1941–1945*, George F. Nafziger (1998)

Sharp, Charles S., *The Deadly Beginning: Soviet Tank, Mechanized, Motorized Divisions and Tank Brigades of 1940–1942*, George F. Nafziger (1995)

Zaloga, Steven J. & Grandsen, James, *The Eastern Front: Armour Camouflage and Markings, 1941 to 1945*, Arms & Armour Press, London (1989)

Zaloga, Steven J. & Ness, Leland S., *Red Army Handbook: 1939–1945*, Sutton Publishing, Barnsley (1998)

Zaloga, Steven J. & Grandsen, James, *Soviet Tanks and Combat Vehicles of World War Two*, Arms & Armor Press, London (1984)

Zaloga, Steven J., *Soviet Lend-Lease Tanks of World War II* (New Vanguard 247), Osprey, Oxford (2017)

Axis tanks and forces

Battistelli, Pier Paolo, *Panzer Divisions: The Eastern Front 1941–43* (Battle Orders 35), Osprey, Oxford (2008)

Doyle, Hilary & Jentz, Thomas L., *Panzerkampfwagen IV Ausf. G, H and J 1942–45* (New Vanguard 39), Osprey, Oxford (2001)

Jentz, Thomas L., ed., *Panzertruppen: The Complete Guide to the Creation & Combat Employment of Germany's Tank Force, 1933–1942*, Schiffer Military History, Atglen PA (1996)

Klapdor, Ewald, *Viking Panzers: The German 5th SS Tank Regiment in the East in World War II*, Stackpole Books, Mechanicsburg (2011)

McNab, Chris, *Hitler's Tanks: German Panzers of World War II*, Osprey, Oxford (2020)

Rebentisch, Ernst, *The Combat History of the 23rd Panzer Division in World War II*, Stackpole Books, Mechanicsburg (2012)

Veterans of the 3rd Panzer Division, *Armored Bear: The German 3rd Panzer Division in World War II: Volume I*, Stackpole Books, Mechanicsburg (2013)

INDEX

References to illustrations, tables, or information in captions are shown in **bold.**

35(t)s tanks 12, 18, 22
38(t)s tanks 12, 18, 22, 40

A17 Tetrarch tanks 27–28, **28**, **42–43**
Axis allies 37, 40
  1st Slovak Mobile (Fast) Division 10, **16–17**, 18, **19**, 40

Baku oil field 4, 28–29, 34, 44
BT tanks 18
  BT-5 21, 22
  BT-7 21, 22, **38**
Budyonny, Marshall Semyon 30–31, **31**

Caucasus campaign
  analysis 44–45
  Hitler's drive for oil 28–37
  retreat 37–39
  stalemate 39–44
Czech tanks 10, 12, **16**, 18, 22, 40

German armed forces
  1st Mountain Division 34, **37**
  3rd Panzer Division 6, 7, **16–17**, 29, 31, 34, 36, 39
  4th Panzer Regiment **6**, **37**
  5th Panzer Battalion **7**, **10**, **39**
  6th Panzer Regiment **6**, **16–17**, **37**
  13th Panzer Division 6, 7, **14**, 31, 34, 36–37, **37**, 39–40, 44, 45
  16th Motorized Division 7–8, **10**, 31, 34, **37**, 44
  16th Panzer Division 6, 8
  22nd Panzer Division 6, 18, 31
  23rd Panzer Division 6, 7, **8–9**, **16**, 29, 30, **31–33**, 34, **34–35**, 36, 37, **38**
  50th Infantry Division 39, 41
  101st Light Division 44
  111th Infantry Division 36
  116th Panzer Battalion 8, **10**
  191st Assault Gun Battalion **14–15**, 44
  201st Panzer Regiment **6**, **8–9**, 30, **31–33**, **37**
  503rd Heavy Tank Battalion 19
  525th Anti-Tank Battalion 40
  Army Group A 7, 12, 16, **19**, 28, 29–31, **30**, 36, **36**, 37, 39, 44–45
  Army Group B 7, 11–12, 19, 28, 31, 44
  Army Group Center 6, 31
  Army Group South 6, 7, 10, 11, **16**, 28, 45
  doctrine and organization 5–10, 44–45
  First Panzer Army 7, **8**, 10, **14**, **16**, 18, 29, 31, **31–33**, 34, 36, 39, 44, 45
  Grossdeutschland Motorized divisions 31
  motorcycle battalions 30, 31
  motorized infantry *Kampfgruppen* 31
  Seventeenth Army 7, 10, **14**, 29, **31**, 34, **34–35**, **37**, 39–41, 44, 45
  Sixth Army 12, 19, 37, 44
  SS Wiking Motorized Division 7, **7–9**, **10**, 31, 34, 36, 37, **37**, **39**
  technical factors 12–20
Great Britain, Lend-Lease tanks 12, 21, **25**, 26–28, 28, 38, **38**, 40, **42–43**
Grozny oil field 4, 28–29, 34, 36, 44

Kerch Straits 39, 39–41, 45
Kharkov **4**, 7, 11, 29
Kuban Bridgehead 39–44, 45
KV-1 tanks 11, 12, 14, 16, 18, 19, 21, 24, 42

Lend-Lease tanks 5, **11**, 12, 16, **20**, 21, 25–28
  Caucasus campaign 31, **34–35**, 36, 38, **38**, 40–41, **42–43**
List, Field Marshall Wilhelm 29, 34, 36, **37**, 44
LT-35 tanks **16**, 18, **19**
LT-38 tanks **16**, 18
LT-40 tanks **16–17**, **19**

M3 Lee tanks (M3S) **11**, 16, 12, **20**, 27, **27**, **34–35**, 41
M3 Stuart tanks (M3L) **11**, 12, 16, 21, 26, **26**, 27, **34–35**, 38, **38**, 40–41, **42**
M4 Sherman tanks 26
Maikop oil field 4, 28–29, 31, 34, 44
Malinovsky, General Rodin 29–30
Marder II 19–20, 40
Martynovka 30, **31–33**
Matilda tanks (Mark II) 21, 26
Model, Field Marshall Walter 7

Novorossiysk 40–41, **42**, **45**

oil fields 4, 6, 28–29, 31, 34, 36, 39, 44
Operation *Barbarossa* 5, 7, 10, 11, **16**, 18, 21, 25
Operation *Edelweiss* 28–29, 28–31, 44
Operation *Fall Blau* **4**, **6**, 7, 8, **10**, 11, 13, 16, 29
Operation *Typhoon* 7
Operation *Uranus* 12, 37
Operation *Wintergewitter* **8**, 37
Operation *Zitadelle* 18, 40, 45
Ordzhonikidze **22**, 36–37
Ozerekya Bay **34–35**, 40–41

paint schemes **8–9**, **16–17**, **22**, **23**, **42–43**
PzBfWg command tanks 6, **6**, **8–9**, **10**, 20, 37, 40
PzKpfw I 12, 20
PzKpfw II 6, **6**, **10**, 12, 16, 18, **18**, 19, 22
  Ausf.F **16–17**
  Caucasus campaign **37**, 39–40
PzKpfw III 6, **6**, **7**, **8–9**, **10**, 12–14, **12**, **13**, 20, 22, **22**
  Ausf.D 20
  Ausf.E 13, 20
  Ausf.F 14
  Ausf.H 20
  Ausf.J 14, **20**
  Ausf.L **8–9**
  Caucasus campaign **37**, 39–40, **39**, 40, 44
PzKpfw IV 6, **6**, **8**, **10**, 12, 13, 14–16, **14–15**, 22, **22**
  Ausf.F **31–33**
  Ausf.F2 **13**, **14–15**, 16, **16**, **20**
  Ausf.G **14**, 16, **31–33**
  Caucasus campaign **37**, 40, 44
PzKpfw V Panther 18–19
PzKpfw VI Tiger I 13, 18–19, **19**

Red Army
  2nd Tank Brigade 36–37, 38
  5th Guards Brigade 36–37, **38**, **42–43**
  6th Guards Regiment 42
  9th Army 41
  11th NKVD division 31
  15th Tank Brigade 38
  17th Cavalry Corps 30
  37th Army 36
  47th Army **38**
  52nd Tank Brigade 36, 38
  56th Army **38**, 44
  62nd Naval Infantry Brigade 36
  62nd OTB **38**
  63rd Tank Brigade 38
  92nd Tank Brigade 41, 44
  110th Cavalry Division 29–30
  115th Cavalry Divisions 29–30
  126th OTB 34, **38**
  132nd OTB 41
  135th Tank Brigade 29–30, **31–33**
  140th Tank Brigade 38
  151st Tank Brigade **22–23**, 28, **28**, **38**, **42–43**, 44
  155th Tank Brigade 29–30, **31–33**
  207th Tank Brigade **10**, **22–23**, 38
  225th Tank Regiment 38
  249th Tank Battalions 36
  257th Tank Regiment 44
  258th OTB 36, **38**
  266th OTB 38
  305th Naval Infantry Battalion 41
  562nd OTB 38
  563rd OTB **34–35**, 36, **38**, 40
  564th OTB **38**
  Black Sea Group 38, 39
  doctrine and organization 10–12, 44–45
  Maikop Tank Brigade 30
  North Caucasus Front 40
  Northern Group 38, 38–39
  Southern Front 12, 29–31
  Tank Group Filippov 12, 38
  Tank Group Lobanov 12, 38–39
  technical factors 21–28
  Transcaucasus Front **10**, **22–23**, **26**, **28**, 40
Rostov 28–29, 37, 39

Sd.Kfz. 265 *Panzerbefehlswagen* 20
Stalin, Josef 21, 30, 40
StuG III assault gun 14, **14–15**, 19, **22**
  Caucasus campaign **30**, **31**, 34, 40, 41, 42, 44, **44**, 45

T-26 tanks **10**, 11, 18, **21**, 21–22, **22–23**
  Caucasus campaign 34, **38**, 40
T-34 tanks **4**, 11, 12, 14, 16, **20**, 21, 22–24, **22–25**
  Caucasus campaign 30, **31–33**, 36, 38, **38**, 40, **41**, 42, **45**
T-38 tanks 40
T-40 tanks 24–25
T-60 tanks 11, 12, 18, 21, 24–25
  Caucasus campaign 29, 38, **38**, 40
T-70 tanks 18, 21, 25, 30, **31–33**, 38
Terek River **8**, **16**, 34, 36, 37, **39**, 44

United States, Lend-Lease tanks **11**, 12, 16, **20**, 21, 26–27, **26–27**, **34–35**, 38, 38, 40–41, **42**

Valentine tanks (Mark III) 12, 21, **25**, 26, 38, **38**, 40, **42–43**
von Kleist, Gen Ewald 7, 29, 34, 36–37, 39, 45
von Manstein, Erich **8**, 39